W9-ATY-330

Country ABCs

New Zealand ABCs

A Book About the People and Places of New Zealand

Written by Holly Schroeder   •   Illustrated by Claudia Wolf

Special thanks to our advisers for their expertise:
Giselle M. Byrnes, Ph.D.
Senior Lecturer in New Zealand History
Victoria University of Wellington, New Zealand

Susan Kesselring, M.A., Literacy Educator
Rosemount-Apple Valley-Eagan (Minnesota) School District

PICTURE WINDOW BOOKS
Minneapolis, Minnesota

Managing Editor: Bob Temple
Creative Director: Terri Foley
Editor: Nadia Higgins
Editorial Adviser: Andrea Cascardi
Copy Editor: Laurie Kahn
Designer: John Moldstad
Page production: Picture Window Books
The illustrations in this book were prepared digitally.

Picture Window Books
5115 Excelsior Boulevard
Suite 232
Minneapolis, MN 55416
1-877-845-8392
www.picturewindowbooks.com

Copyright © 2004 by Picture Window Books
All rights reserved. No part of this book may be reproduced without written permission from the publisher. The publisher
takes no responsibility for the use of any of the materials or methods described in this book, nor for the products thereof.

Printed in the United States of America.

Library of Congress Cataloging-in-Publication Data
Schroeder, Holly.
New Zealand ABCs : a book about the people and places of New Zealand /
written by Holly Schroeder ; illustrated by Claudia Wolf.
p. cm. — (Country ABCs)
Summary: An alphabetical exploration of the people, geography, animals,
plants, history, and culture of New Zealand.
Includes bibliographical references and index.
ISBN 1-4048-0178-2 (reinforced lib. bdg.)
1. New Zealand—Juvenile literature. [1. New Zealand. 2. Alphabet.]
I. Wolf, Claudia, ill. II. Title. III. Series.
DU408 .S37 2004
993—dc22
2003016524

3MBL000016433C

G'day! That's how New Zealanders greet one another in English.

Tena koe! (TEN-uh kway) And that is how they greet one another in Maori, New Zealand's second official language.

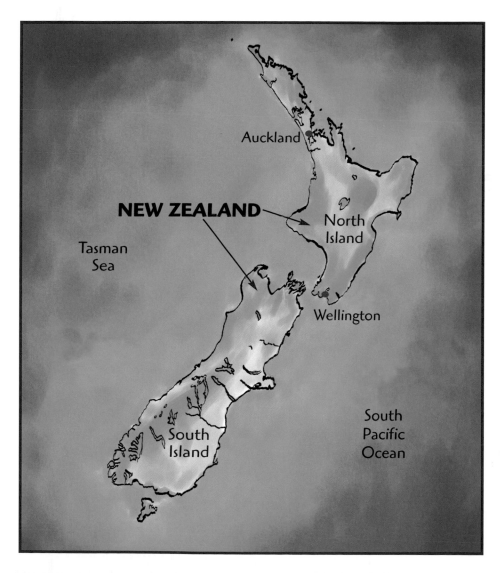

New Zealand is an island country south of Asia. It lies in the South Pacific Ocean. About 4 million people live in New Zealand. It ranks 121st in world population.

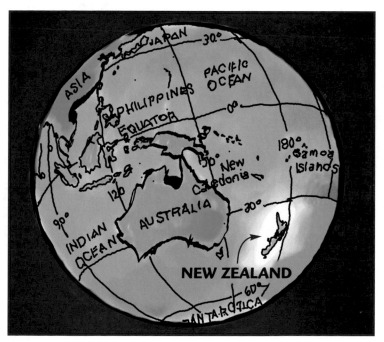

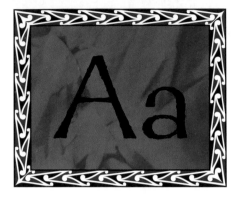

A is for Aotearoa
(ah-or-te-ah-ROAR).

About 1,200 years ago, a group of Pacific islanders left their land and paddled their canoes south. They came upon a large island where no people were living. They named their new home Aotearoa. That means "land of the long white cloud." Today the official name of the country is New Zealand. It is also referred to as Aotearoa, out of respect for those first settlers.

FAST FACT: *The original settlers, the Maori, called their large canoes* waka.

B is for Britain.

New Zealand has close ties to Great Britain. Captain James Cook, a British explorer, sailed to New Zealand in his ship *Endeavour.* In 1769, he became the first European to land in the country. Eventually, many more British settlers arrived and took over the country from the Maori natives. Today New Zealand is still a member of the British Commonwealth, although it has its own government.

FAST FACT: Great Britain's Queen Elizabeth is still the official head of New Zealand's government. The queen has little real power, but she plays an important symbolic role.

5

C is for carving.

The original settlers, the Maori, carved the canoes that allowed them to travel to their new home. The Maori have since become famous for their beautiful wood carvings. Maori artists seldom carve a straight line. They prefer detailed, swirling patterns.

6

D is for dollar.

The New Zealand dollar is the country's basic unit of money. It is made up of 100 cents. New Zealand dollars come in $5, $10, $20, $50, and $100 bills. Coins range from five cents to two dollars.

FAST FACT: *New Zealand has no pennies. This saves people from having to deal with a lot of small coins.*

E is for earthquakes.

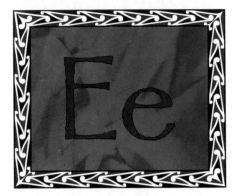

In a typical year, New Zealand has about 100 earthquakes strong enough to be felt. The worst one was in 1931, when 256 people were killed. New Zealand has some of the strictest laws in the world about how houses can be built. Builders have to be very careful to design homes that will last through bad earthquakes.

FAST FACT: *In addition to earthquakes, New Zealand has many volcanoes. Mount Ruapehu most recently erupted in 1997.*

F is for flag.

New Zealand's present flag was adopted in 1902. In the upper left corner is a small British flag. This is to show that New Zealand is still a part of the British Commonwealth. The four stars stand for the Southern Cross, the stars that shine most brightly in the New Zealand sky.

G is for geysers.

New Zealand is one of only three countries in the world that have geysers. The other two countries are the United States and Iceland. Geysers are explosions of hot water from deep inside the earth. They are caused when water seeps down into pools of hot rock. The water heats up quickly and then bursts up out of the ground.

H is for hemisphere.

New Zealand is in the southern half of the globe. We call this the Southern Hemisphere. Countries in the Southern Hemisphere have opposite seasons to those in the Northern Hemisphere. When it's winter in the North, it's summer in the South. Kids in New Zealand have their summer vacation in December and January.

FAST FACT: New Zealand is just west of an imaginary line running north and south on the globe. This line is called the international date line. It marks where each day begins. New Zealanders are among the first to see each new day dawn.

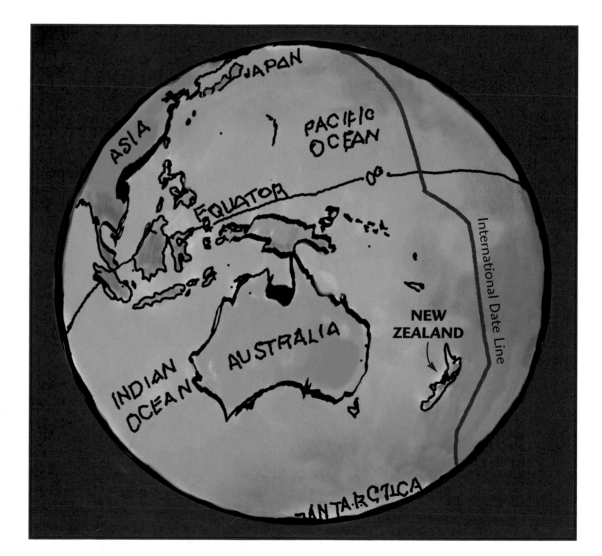

I is for islands.

Two huge islands, the North Island and the South Island, make up most of New Zealand. Scattered around these, 141 smaller landmasses poke up out of the vast oceans that surround this island nation.

These are some of the many little islands that make up New Zealand.

J is for jumping.

Thrill seekers from around the world travel to New Zealand to bungee jump off tall towers, bridges, and cliffs. They strap long rubber cords to their ankles, and then leap. Jumpers bounce up and down like yo-yos before they are pulled back up to safety.

FAST FACT: People in Polynesia have been doing a sport like bungee jumping for centuries. But it was a New Zealander who invented bungee jumping as we know it today.

13

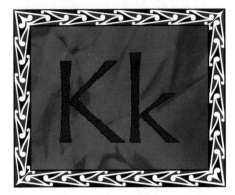

K is for kiwi.

The kiwi is a round, fuzzy bird that can't fly. It lives only in New Zealand. New Zealanders must have a sense of humor. They like to call themselves Kiwis, after the strange bird that lives among them.

FAST FACT: *Kiwifruit was developed by New Zealand fruit growers. They named the brown, fuzzy fruit after their favorite bird.*

L is for Lake Taupo (TOE-poe).

Lake Taupo is New Zealand's largest lake. The majestic lake fills a crater that was made by one of the biggest volcanic eruptions in history.

FAST FACT: *One popular thing to do at Lake Taupo is to go for a helicopter ride and view the scenery.*

M is for Maori.

The Maori were the first people to live in New Zealand. But at one point in the country's history, it looked as if the Maori culture would die out. Since the 1970s, the Maori people have worked hard to keep their heritage alive. Today, the Maori make up only 14% of the population. But their language, values, and customs have become an important part of New Zealand culture.

Maori in traditional dress

N is for nuclear-free zone.

In 1984, the New Zealand government passed an important law. The law said the country would not let any ships carrying nuclear weapons into its ports. At times, the law has created problems with other countries. But New Zealanders refuse to change the law. They see it as an important stand for peace in their part of the world.

O is for ocean.

The ocean has acted like a big fence around New Zealand. It has kept many of the country's plants and animals from growing anywhere else in the world. Of the 2,000 plants that first grew here, 1,500 don't grow anywhere else.

FAST FACT: *Before people brought animals from other lands, New Zealand had no mammals except for two kinds of bats.*

P is for parliament.

People in New Zealand don't vote for a president. Instead, they elect 120 members of parliament. Members in parliament elect the prime minister, who is the country's most powerful ruler. The members also make the country's laws.

Members of parliament meet at this building, called the Beehive.

Q is for Queenstown.

Queenstown offers all kinds of attractions for New Zealand's many tourists. Adventure seekers can go rafting down a wild river. History buffs can visit historic buildings from New Zealand's gold-mining days. Tourism is one of New Zealand's most important industries. The government is working to bring even more visitors to Queenstown and other tourist spots.

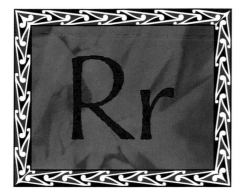

R is for rugby.

This sport is a combination of soccer and American-style football. It is also New Zealanders' favorite game. Members of the national team, the All Blacks, are considered national heroes. Children often begin playing rugby at age five, or even younger.

S is for sheep.

From a distance, herds of sheep sometimes look like patches of snow against New Zealand's green land. The country has more than 39 million sheep. That's about 10 sheep for each person. New Zealand is the world's third largest producer of wool.

T is for the Treaty of Waitangi (why-TANG-ee).

This treaty was an agreement between the Maori chiefs and the British. Signed in 1840, it made Great Britain's Queen Victoria the leader of New Zealand. The treaty has caused many disagreements between the Maori and the *Pakeha* (white) people. The New Zealand government recognizes that the Maori have been treated unfairly. It has returned some land to the Maori people.

U is for umu.

Maori cook special feasts in *umus*, or underground ovens. They steam packets of meat and vegetables in these shallow pits covered with wet towels and dirt. Cooking in an umu takes the whole day. But a big group of guests makes this special meal worth the trouble.

V is for voting.

In 1893, New Zealand became the first country in the world to allow women to vote. It was also the first country to give pension checks to retired people. Most people in New Zealand are happy with their government. They are proud of their country's forward-thinking policies.

In 1999, Helen Clark became the first woman to be elected prime minister.

W is for Wellington.

When New Zealand was first settled by the British, they put the capital in Auckland. Auckland is far north in the North Island. The people in the South Island said it was too far away. So the capital was moved to Wellington. Wellington is right in the middle of the country.

FAST FACT: *Most people in New Zealand live in cities in the North Island.*

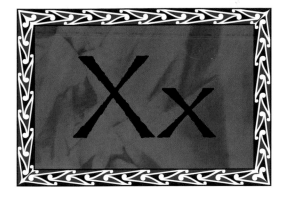

X is for extinct.

Sometimes all animals of a certain kind die. When that happens, we say that animal is extinct. New Zealand was once home to the largest bird in the world, called a moa. It grew up to 12 feet (3½ meters) tall. When people came to New Zealand, they hunted the moa and destroyed its habitat. The moa has been extinct for hundreds of years.

FAST FACT: Many other kinds of birds, as well as about 10% of the country's native plants, are becoming extinct. People in New Zealand are working hard to save these plants and birds.

27

Y is for yacht.

The most famous yacht race in the world takes place in New Zealand. The boat that won the first race, in 1851, was called *America.* Since then, the race has been known as the America's Cup. New Zealand's boat *Black Magic* won the race in both 1995 and 2000.

FAST FACT: *New Zealand's biggest city, Auckland, is known as the City of Sails. About one out of every four families in Auckland owns a boat.*

Z is for Godzone.

Many New Zealanders affectionately call their country Godzone. Godzone is short for God's Own Country. New Zealanders say their country is so beautiful, it must be God's favorite place.

New Zealand in Brief

Official Name: New Zealand

Capital: Wellington (345,000 people)

Official languages: English and Maori

Population: 3,997,000

People: 74% *Pakeha* (white of European descent), 14% Maori, 6% Polynesian, 6% Asian

Religion: Most people (81%) are Christian.

Education: free for children between 5 and 19; required for children between 6 and 16

Major holidays: Waitangi Day (February 6); ANZAC Day (April 25); Queen's Birthday (June); Labor Day (October); Boxing Day (December 26)

Driving: People drive on the left side of the road.

Climate: mostly warm, comfortable temperatures; plenty of rain and little snow

Area: 103,883 square miles (269,056 square kilometers) — about the size of the state of Colorado

Highest point: Mount Cook, 12,349 feet (3,764 meters)

Lowest point: Pacific Ocean, sea level

Type of government: parliamentary democracy; independent member of British Commonwealth

Head of government: prime minister

Major industries: food processing, machinery, banking, mining, tourism

Natural resources: natural gas, iron ore, gold, timber, coal

Major agricultural products: wool, beef, dairy products, fruits, vegetables

Chief exports: wool, meat, dairy products

Money: New Zealand dollar

New Zealand Words and Phrases

bloke, mate . . . . .guy
chippies . . . . .potato chips
dairy .a convenience store
Good on ya, mate! . . . . .Congratulations!
ice block . . . . .Popsicle
loo .bathroom
pudding . . . . .dessert
spotcha . . . . .see you later
ta . . . . .thanks
togs .bathing suit
wonky . . . . .crooked
yonks . . . . .a long time ago

Say It in Maori

yes . . . .*ae* (eye)
no . . . .*kaore* (ka-OW-ri)
welcome . . . .*haere mai* (HA-ere my)
good-bye . . . .*haere ra* (HA-ere ra)
food/eat . . . .*kai* (kie; rhymes with pie)
How are you? . . . .*Kei te pehea koe?* (keh teh PEH-ha kway)
hello (informal) . . . .*kia ora* (KEE-a ORE-ah)
water . . . .*wai* (why)

Glossary

British Commonwealth—a group of countries that have been ruled by Great Britain at some point in history
crater—a wide, bowl-shaped dip in the earth
Maori—the first people to live in New Zealand; the language of the Maori people
mammals—a category of warm-blooded animals. Mammals are covered with spines, fur, or hair, and they nurse their young.
nuclear weapons—the most dangerous kind of weapons in the world
pension—money the government sends to retired people
treaty—a written agreement between countries or groups of people. A treaty is signed by the people's leaders.

To Learn More

At the Library

Beck, Katie. *The Moas.* Kansas City, Mo.:
  Landmark Editions, 1999.

Landau, Elaine. *Australia and New Zealand.* New York:
  Children's Press, 1999.

Ryan, Patrick. *New Zealand.* Chanhassen, Minn.:
  Child's World, 1999.

Theunissen, Steve. *The Maori of New Zealand.* Minneapolis:
  Lerner Publications Co., 2003.

Ylvisaker, Anne. *The Pacific Ocean.* Mankato, Minn.:
  Bridgestone Books, 2003.

On the Web

Fact Hound

Fact Hound offers a safe, fun way to find Web sites related to this book.
All of the sites on Fact Hound have been researched by our staff.
http://www.facthound.com

1. Visit the Fact Hound home page.
2. Enter a search word related to this book,
   or type in this special code: 1404801782.
3. Click on the FETCH IT button.

Your trusty Fact Hound will fetch the best sites for you!

Index